Corpse Talk
by
Adam Murphy

For Lisa

Corpse Talk: Season 1
is a
DAVID FICKLING BOOK

First published in Great Britain in 2014 by
David Fickling Books,
31 Beaumont Street,
Oxford, OX1 2NP

Text and Illustrations © Adam Murphy, 2014

978-1-910200-01-8

1 3 5 7 9 10 8 6 4 2

David Fickling Books supports the Forest Stewardship Council
(FSC), the leading international forest certification organisation.
All our titles that are printed on Greenpeace-approved
FSC-certified paper carry the FSC logo.

FSC
www.fsc.org

MIX
Paper from
responsible sources
FSC® C015140

DAVID FICKLING BOOKS Reg. No. 8340307

A CIP catalogue record for this book is available
from the British Library

Printed and bound in Great Britain
by Polestar Stones.

In the Guest Graveyard this Season...

Digging up the Bodies

AND HERE TO GET THE SHOW OFF TO A **FLYING START** IS QUEEN OF THE AIR, **AMELIA EARHART**!

HELLO, EVERYONE!

AMELIA, YOU CAPTURED THE WORLD'S IMAGINATION WITH YOUR PIONEERING FLIGHTS. CAN YOU TELL US WHEN YOUR LOVE OF FLYING BEGAN?

WELL, WHEN I WAS A LITTLE GIRL, MY UNCLE NICEY BUILT A **ROLLERCOASTER RAMP** FOR US IN THE BACK YARD...

"PIDGE" LITTLE SISTER

CRACK!

← "JAMES FEROCIOUS" (DOG)

OH, **PIDGE**! IT'S JUST LIKE **FLYING**!

I LOVED THE FEELING OF SOARING THROUGH THE AIR! BUT BACK THEN, LITTLE GIRLS WEREN'T **SUPPOSED** TO HAVE ADVENTURES...

IN FACT, BY THE TIME I WENT TO THE **AIR SHOW**, I'D FORGOTTEN ALL ABOUT IT...

THAT WAS WHEN THE PILOT DECIDED TO GIVE US A FRIGHT!

BUT I WAS NOT AFRAID...

I LOVED IT! AFTER THAT, I TOOK LESSONS AND STARTED FLYING AS MUCH AS I COULD!

WOO!

UH, CAN YOU FOCUS PLEASE?

BUT AT THAT TIME, FLYING WASN'T CONSIDERED **LADYLIKE**.

AVIATION CLUB

NO GIRLS ALLOWED!

AH, BUT THAT ALL CHANGED WHEN YOU BECAME...

THE FACE OF FEMALE AVIATION!

YES, WELL, THEY WANTED A WOMAN TO FLY ACROSS THE ATLANTIC, SO THEY ASKED ME! I WAS JUST THERE FOR PROMOTION; I DIDN'T EVEN FLY THE PLANE...

BUT THE NEWSPAPERS **LOVED** YOU!

COVER GIRL!

ROLE MODEL!

AUTHOR!

FASHION DESIGNER!

YOU HAD IT ALL!

BUT MOST IMPORTANTLY, ALL THIS MEANT THAT NOW I COULD FLY WHENEVER I WANTED.

AND YOU DIDN'T STOP THERE...

CERTAINLY NOT! I DIDN'T LIKE THAT I'D JUST BEEN A PASSENGER ON THAT TRANSATLANTIC FLIGHT...

SO IN 1929 I BECAME THE **FIRST WOMAN** TO FLY IT, SOLO AND UNAIDED!

I WANTED TO PROVE THAT WOMEN HAVE AS MUCH WILL AND COURAGE AND DETERMINATION AS MEN.

WELL, YOU CERTAINLY PROVED THAT WITH YOUR **ROUND-THE-WORLD** FLIGHT...

BUT IT WAS **SO DANGEROUS**! WHY DO IT?!

WHAT CAN I SAY?

I KNEW THE RISKS; I JUST WANTED TO DO IT. AND, IF I FAILED, IT WOULD JUST BE A CHALLENGE TO OTHERS...

AND THIS WAS YOUR **LAST** FLIGHT, WASN'T IT?

YES. WE RAN OUT OF FUEL AT SEA AND WERE **NEVER SEEN AGAIN**.

STILL TO THIS DAY, NO ONE KNOWS WHAT HAPPENED TO YOU! IN FACT, EVEN AS WE SPEAK, RESEARCH IS GOING ON TO FIND YOUR LAST RESTING PLACE!

AND I'D SURE HATE TO SPOIL THEIR FUN!

WELL, GOTTA FLY!

I GUESS WE'LL LEAVE THIS STORY STILL **CLOUDED** IN MYSTERY!

What a Drag!

When Anne first set to sea, she fell in love with a handsome young pirate. She revealed her secret to him — that she was actually a woman in disguise — but was disappointed to discover that **he** was actually Mary Read, **another** lady pirate, who was **also** in disguise!

It was shortly after this that they decided it would probably be easier to just go around dressed as women.

JOAN OF ARC

THIS WEEK, MY GUEST IS A TRUE **VISIONARY**! IT'S THE **MAID OF ORLEANS, JOAN OF ARC**!

'ALLO!

JOAN, FRANCE WAS IN A PRETTY BAD WAY WHEN YOU WERE A LITTLE GIRL...

YES, IT WAS **HORRIFIC** TIMES.

FOR ALMOST A CENTURY, THE ENGLISH ARMY HAD BEEN **TERRORISING** THE COUNTRYSIDE, BURNING, LOOTING AND KILLING.

THE FRENCH ARMY, TIRED AND DEFEATED, HAD BEEN LOSING FOR SO LONG, THAT THEY DIDN'T BELIEVE THEY COULD WIN...

YOU WERE JUST A **FARMER'S DAUGHTER**, WHAT COULD **YOU** DO ABOUT IT?

BY MYSELF, NOT MUCH.

BUT, WHEN I WAS 12, **ST MICHAEL** AND **ST CATHERINE** APPEARED TO ME IN A VISION. THEY TOLD ME **I** WAS TO CHASE THE ENGLISH OUT OF FRANCE, AND CROWN THE RIGHTFUL KING.

WAIT. YOU DIDN'T REALLY **SEE** THEM, RIGHT? IT WAS YOUR **IMAGINATION**...

OF COURSE. THAT IS HOW THE MESSAGES OF GOD COME TO US.

ANYWAY, I SET OFF TO MEET THE WOULD-BE KING AND ANNOUNCED MY MISSION...

GOD HAS SENT ME!

HE COULD **ONLY** BE CROWNED AT **REIMS** CATHEDRAL, AND THE ENGLISH HELD REIMS...

BUT THE ARMY WAS IN TATTERS. HOW DID YOU TAKE THESE **SAD LOSERS** AND TURN THEM INTO **FIGHTING FRENCHMEN?!**

THEY HAD LOST THEIR FAITH, THE POOR LAMBS! I TAUGHT THEM THAT THEY WERE **SOLDIERS OF GOD**!

I MADE THEM ALL STOP SWEARING (IT'S BAD FOR THE SOUL).

AND WHEN WE WENT INTO **BATTLE**, I WAS RIGHT THERE AT THEIR HEAD!

WITH YOUR NEWLY MOTIVATED TROOPS, YOU **ROUTED** THE ENGLISH AND SET THE KING ON HIS THRONE. IT WAS YOUR **TRIUMPH!**

IT WAS MY **DOWNFALL!**

THE KING GOT WHAT HE WANTED - HE DIDN'T NEED ME ANY MORE. BUT THE ENGLISH WERE STILL IN FRANCE!

I KEPT FIGHTING, BUT WITHOUT THE KING'S SUPPORT I DIDN'T HAVE ENOUGH SOLDIERS.

ABANDONED BY THOSE I'D HELPED MOST, I WAS CAPTURED AND IMPRISONED.

BUT THE WORST WAS YET TO COME! THE CHURCH I LOVED SO MUCH DECIDED THAT MY VISIONS WERE **EVIL!**

THEY HAD A **TERRIBLE PUNISHMENT** FOR THAT!

BUT YOU HAD A WAY OUT, RIGHT? YOU COULD JUST SAY YOU MADE IT ALL UP!

I DID! I WAS **AFRAID**, GOD FORGIVE ME, AND I LIED. I SAID WHATEVER THEY WANTED...

BUT I COULDN'T GO THROUGH WITH IT! MY VISIONS WERE **TRUE** AND **GOOD**! BETTER TO DIE FOR THE TRUTH THAN TO LIVE A LIE!

ON THE 30TH MAY, 1431, I WAS **BURNED TO DEATH**.

COME ON, IT'S OK. YOU STILL NEED A FUNNY ENDING FOR YOUR COMIC.

HOW ABOUT THIS... "HOLY SMOKES!"

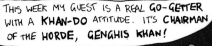
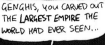

ALEXANDER VON HUMBOLDT

MY GUEST THIS WEEK IS A **FORCE OF NATURE!** IT'S EXPLORER, GEOGRAPHER, CARTOGRAPHER, GEOLOGIST, BOTANIST, SOCIOLOGIST AND VOLCANOLOGIST **ALEXANDER VON HUMBOLDT!**

HI!

ALEXANDER, YOU'RE BEST KNOWN FOR YOUR SCIENTIFIC EXPLORATIONS IN SOUTH AMERICA AND THE INCREDIBLE NUMBER OF DISCOVERIES THAT YOU MADE...

IN YOUR FIVE-YEAR EXPEDITION, YOU DISCOVERED **3,500** NEW SPECIES, THE MOST BY ANYONE EVER ON A SINGLE TRIP!

YES, IT WAS **GLORIOUS!** I COLLECTED 60,000 SPECIMENS, AND MADE OVER **400** DRAWINGS.

I ALSO RECORDED A **STUPENDOUS** AMOUNT OF **INVALUABLE** DATA ON THE WEATHER, SOIL, ROCKS, FOSSILS, RIVERS, OCEANS, ATMOSPHERE AND MAGNETIC FIELDS!

NATURALLY, I BROUGHT SOME SCIENTIFIC INSTRUMENTS...

A TELESCOPE WITH AN ARM TO AFFIX IT TO TREES

TWO ELECTROMETERS FOR MEASURING THE ELECTRICITY OF THE ATMOSPHERE

A POCKET SEXTANT FOR FIXING YOUR POSITION EVEN IN A BOAT OR ON HORSEBACK

A CYANOMETER FOR MEASURING THE BLUENESS OF THE SKY

AND MANY OTHERS; PLUS MY **LIBRARY** OF COURSE. AND CASES FOR ALL OF MY SPECIMENS...

GOOD GRIEF! HOW DID YOU **CARRY** IT ALL?!

WELL, LUCKILY I HAD SOME **ASSISTANCE**...

IT SOUNDS VERY EXCITING, BUT TRAVELLING THROUGH THE JUNGLE MUST HAVE BEEN **DANGEROUS!**

YES, WELL, THERE **WERE** JAGUARS...

PIRANHAS, CROCODILES...

AND THE WORST DANGER OF ALL... **ANTS!**

I TRIED BURNING THEM, SMOKING THEM, FLOODING THEM, STOMPING THEM...

...BUT THEY STILL MADE OFF WITH MY PRICELESS **PLANTS!**

MY **SPECIMENS!**

YOU STILL MANAGED TO AMASS AN IMPRESSIVE COLLECTION!

YES, BUT IT'S MORE THAN JUST COLLECTING SPECIMENS...

I WANTED TO UNDERSTAND WHAT I CALLED "HARMONY IN NATURE"— THE INVISIBLE FORCES THAT CONNECT PLANTS, ANIMALS AND THEIR ENVIRONMENT.

FOR EXAMPLE, I WAS THE FIRST TO REALISE THAT SIMILAR HABITATS EXIST ALL AROUND THE WORLD BASED ON HOW WARM OR COOL IT IS...

YOU RETURNED TO EUROPE A **CELEBRITY!** IT'S SAID THAT, AFTER NAPOLEON, YOU WERE THE MOST FAMOUS MAN IN THE WORLD!

I MET HIM ONCE. I THINK HE WAS JEALOUS...

YOU COLLECT **PLANTS?**

PFF... SO DOES MY **WIFE!**

BUT NO ONE, NOT EVEN **NAPOLEON,** CAN CLAIM TO HAVE AS MANY THINGS NAMED AFTER HIM!

A PENGUIN — A SQUID — AN OCEAN CURRENT — A BAY — A DRY LAKE BED — THREE COUNTIES — FOUR UNIVERSITIES, TWO COLLEGES AND NINE SCHOOLS — A LUNAR SEA — TWO MOUNTAIN RANGES — A SKUNK — A GLACIER — THREE PARKS — AN ASTEROID — THREE STREETS — A RIVER DOLPHIN — TWO MOUNTAINS — TEN TOWNS — FOUR TREES — FOUR PLANTS — A RIVER — A SINKHOLE — A HOTEL

IT'S VERY FLATTERING, BUT I REALLY NEVER WANTED ALL THAT ATTENTION...

NICE TO SEE THAT YOU STAYED **HUMBLE...(DT)!**

MARIE CURIE!

THIS WEEK MY GUEST COMES WITH **GLOWING RECOMMENDATIONS!** IT'S TWO-TIME NOBEL PRIZE WINNER **MARIE CURIE!**

NOW, YOU MIGHT SPOT SOMETHING DIFFERENT ABOUT ME IN THIS EPISODE, AND NO, IT'S NOT MY NEW HAIRCUT

(THANKS FOR NOTICING THOUGH).

MARIE, WITH HER HUSBAND PIERRE, DISCOVERED **RADIATION.** TURNS OUT, IT KILLS <u>YOU</u>...

HENCE THE SUIT.

WE DIDN'T KNOW...

MARIE, TIMES WERE TOUGH IN POLAND WHEN YOU WERE A GIRL...

THAT'S FOR SURE! BACK THEN, THE **RUSSIANS** RULED POLAND...

AND ONE OF THEIR RULES WAS THAT NO POLES WERE ALLOWED TO GET AN **EDUCATION.**

I WASN'T GOING TO LET **THAT** STOP ME! I STUDIED SCIENCE AT A **TOP SECRET UNDERGROUND UNIVERSITY!!**

PASSWORD?

I ♥ SCIENCE

BUT TO LEARN **CUTTING-EDGE** SCIENCE, I HAD TO GO TO THE **NUMBER ONE** UNIVERSITY, AND AT THAT TIME, THAT WAS IN **PARIS!**

I WAS SO POOR, I COULD ONLY AFFORD A TINY ATTIC. IT GOT **SO COLD,** I USED TO SLEEP WITH **ALL MY** CLOTHES ON!

BUT HOW **WONDERFUL,** POOR AND ALONE AS I WAS, TO BE STUDYING IN THE **CAPITAL OF SCIENCE!**

BUT YOU WEREN'T ALONE FOR LONG...

WELL, THAT'S WHERE I MET **PIERRE...**

HE WAS AN **EXTRAORDINARY** MAN, AS TOTALLY DEDICATED TO SCIENCE AS I WAS.

AW! SO **ROMANTIC!**

WE GOT MARRIED AND STARTED ON OUR RESEARCH.

AT THE TIME, **X-RAYS** WERE THE **HOT NEW SCIENCE.**

I SAY!

SPLENDID!

A FRENCH SCIENTIST NAMED **LOUIS BECQUEREL** HAD DISCOVERED **ANOTHER** TYPE OF RAYS GIVEN OFF BY **URANIUM...**

SACRÉ BLEU!

EVEN THOUGH THE WORLD IGNORED HIS DISCOVERY, I WAS **FASCINATED** BY BECQUEREL'S RAYS, AND I MADE AN **AMAZING** DISCOVERY...

SCIENTISTS HAD ALWAYS THOUGHT THAT **ATOMS** WERE THE SMALLEST THINGS THAT EXISTED...

BUT **I** DISCOVERED THAT THE RAYS WERE COMING FROM **INSIDE** THE ATOM!

WE CALLED THE RAYS **"RADIATION".**

AND THEIR DISCOVERY **REVOLUTIONISED** THE WORLD!

THIS WAS THE BIRTH OF **NUCLEAR SCIENCE!**

$E=MC^2$

PIERRE AND I WERE AWARDED OUR FIRST NOBEL PRIZE IN 1903. LIFE WAS GOOD, BUT THEN...

TRAGEDY STRUCK! PIERRE WAS **KILLED** WHEN HE SLIPPED AND FELL UNDER A SPEEDING CART.

MY DEAR PIERRE! HE WAS PROBABLY THINKING ABOUT SCIENCE AND NOT PAYING ATTENTION. MY FRIEND, LOVER AND COMPANION, GONE FOREVER!

BUT LIFE DIDN'T END THERE. I KEPT WORKING ON OUR RESEARCH, AND EVENTUALLY, WAS ABLE TO FOUND A **RESEARCH INSTITUTE** WORTHY OF HIS MEMORY.

AND IT WAS MANY YEARS BEFORE **YOU** DIED, FINALLY SUCCUMBING TO THE EFFECTS OF ALL THAT **RADIATION...**

ALL RIGHT! WE DIDN'T KNOW!

HANG ON, IF YOU'RE **RADIOACTIVE,** DOES THAT MEAN YOU HAVE **AWESOME SUPERPOWERS?!**

WHAT?! NO! THAT'S ONLY TRUE IN **COMIC BOOKS.**

Killer Research

Marie Curie absorbed so much radiation in the course of her work, that even her stuff is radioactive.

To this day her research notebooks are considered too deadly to touch!

EMMELINE PANKHURST

THIS WEEK, MY GUEST IS A DE-**VOTE**-ED CAMPAIGNER FOR **WOMEN'S RIGHTS**! IT'S SUFFRAGETTE LEADER **EMMELINE PANKHURST**!

CHARMED, I'M SURE.

MRS PANKHURST, YOU DEDICATED YOUR LIFE TO WINNING THE RIGHT TO VOTE FOR WOMEN. WHY WAS **THAT** SO IMPORTANT?

WHY WAS IT SO... **YOUNG MAN**! IT'S THE **MOST IMPORTANT** THING!

IN A **DEMOCRACY**, LIKE BRITAIN IS SUPPOSED TO BE, PEOPLE HAVE **ONE WAY** TO HAVE A SAY IN HOW THINGS ARE RUN, AND THAT IS TO **VOTE**.

IF YOU DON'T HAVE A VOTE, NO ONE NEEDS TO LISTEN TO **ANYTHING** YOU SAY. THAT MEANS YOU ARE NOT A **PERSON**, YOU ARE **PROPERTY**.

WOMEN HAD BEEN TRYING FOR **YEARS** TO GET THE VOTE, BUT SINCE THEY DIDN'T **HAVE** THE VOTE, THE GOVERNMENT DIDN'T NEED TO LISTEN TO THEM.

DEAR PRIME MINISTER, WOMEN THINK THAT...

HA HA HA HA

SISTERS! THE GOVERNMENT REFUSES TO LISTEN! THE TIME FOR WORDS IS OVER! NOW IS THE TIME FOR **DEEDS**!

HURRAH!

HEAR HEAR!

WE STARTED BREAKING WINDOWS, LIKE THE PRIME MINISTER'S AT 10 DOWNING STREET.

EGAD!

I USED TO SAY THAT "THE BROKEN WINDOW IS THE MOST PERSUASIVE ARGUMENT IN MODERN POLITICS."

WE CHAINED OURSELVES TO THE RAILINGS OUTSIDE PARLIAMENT.

HOW EMBARRASSING!

FOR **THEM**! THEY COULDN'T IGNORE US THEN!

FROM THERE, WE HIT THEM WHERE IT **REALLY** HURTS. IN THE **GOLF COURSE**!

BURNED WITH ACID

OH, AND PUNCHING POLICEMEN. I ALWAYS LIKED THAT...

BIFF!

NOT **HARD** YOU KNOW... JUST SO WE'D GET ARRESTED.

YOU WANTED TO GET ARRESTED?

WE WANTED TO SHOW THAT WE WERE NOT PREPARED TO BE GOVERNED BY LAWS ON WHICH WE WERE NOT CONSULTED.

SO THEY PUT US IN JAIL. I MYSELF WAS ARRESTED SEVEN OR EIGHT TIMES.

THEY THOUGHT THAT WOULD SHUT US UP! BUT WE CONTINUED TO FIGHT IN THE ONLY WAY LEFT TO US— **A HUNGER STRIKE**!

IT WOULD'VE LOOKED BAD IF WE STARTED **DYING** IN PRISON SO THE GOVERNMENT RELEASED US...

HUNGRY, MRS PANKHURST?

OH, I COULD EAT A HORSE.

AND THEN ARRESTED US AGAIN WHEN WE HAD RECOVERED.

FEELING BETTER, MRS PANKHURST?

=COFF= STILL VERY WEAK, OFFICER...

AND? DID IT WORK?

WELL, WE'LL NEVER REALLY KNOW. IN 1914, THE FIRST WORLD WAR BROKE OUT, AND THAT CHANGED EVERTHING...

WITH ALL THE MEN AWAY FIGHTING, WOMEN HAD TO TAKE THEIR PLACES.

WAS IT OUR ACTIONS, OR WAS IT JUST THE CHANGING WORLD...?

EITHER WAY, WOMEN FINALLY GOT THE RIGHT TO VOTE.

AND I'M SURE ALL THE WOMEN OF BRITAIN WOULD OFFER YOU A **VOTE** OF **THANKS**!

THIS WEEK, PERFECTLY PRESERVED AND ALL THE WAY FROM ANCIENT EGYPT, IT'S BOY KING TUTANKHAMUN!

HEY

KING TUT, YOU BECAME PHARAOH WHEN YOU WERE ONLY EIGHT YEARS OLD! THAT MUST'VE BEEN PRETTY COOL!

WELL, ACTUALLY, NO. IT WAS A ROYAL PAIN!

I HAD TO WEAR ALL THIS HEAVY JEWELLERY AND THIS SILLY, ITCHY FAKE BEARD.

AND I HAD TO SIT STILL FOR HOURS THROUGH ALL THESE BORING RITUALS.

WHAT I REALLY WANTED TO DO WAS PLAY OUTSIDE BUT THEY WOULDN'T LET ME!

BUT THE PHARAOH WAS REVERED AS A GOD! YOU COULD DO WHATEVER YOU WANTED!

WELL, YOU'D THINK SO!

BUT, AS I WAS ALWAYS TOLD: "EVEN A GOD MUST LISTEN TO HIS ADVISERS."

AND WHATEVER THEY "ADVISED", THAT'S WHAT HAPPENED. LIKE WHEN THEY "ADVISED" ME TO RESTORE THE OLD GODS.

THE WHAT NOW?

MY DADDY HAD KICKED OUT ALL THE OLD GODS.

OI! NO FAIR-OH!

BOOT!

HE INVENTED HIS OWN RELIGION, WITH ONLY ONE GOD: THE ATEN.

THIS MADE A LOT OF PEOPLE VERY ANGRY.

SO MY ADVISERS MADE ME ABANDON THE ATEN AND BRING BACK THE OLD GODS.

AW YEAH

GOOD TO BE BACK!

AND THEY MADE ME CHANGE MY NAME! MY DADDY CALLED ME TUTANKHATEN BUT THEY MADE IT TUTANKHAMUN.

THE MAIN GOD WAS AMUN.

MY WIFE HAD TO CHANGE HER NAME TOO. DADDY NAMED HER ANKHESENEPATEN, SO SHE BECAME ANKHESENAMUN.

SO CONFUSING!

WAIT. HOW COME YOUR DAD NAMED YOUR WIFE?

WELL, SHE'S ALSO MY SISTER...

WHAT?

THAT'S NORMAL FOR PHARAOHS. SEE, DADDY WAS A GOD, SO IF HE MARRIED HIS SISTER, I'D BE MORE OF A GOD THAN IF HE MARRIED BENEATH HIM.

BUT, THAT'S JUST SUCH A BAD IDEA. YOU KNOW HOW YOU WERE ALWAYS ILL AND YOU COULDN'T WALK PROPERLY? THAT'S WHY...

WALK SCHMALK! WHO CARES! I WAS A GOD! I HAD SERVANTS TO CARRY ME EVERYWHERE!

IT DIDN'T STOP ME DOING WHAT I LOVED BEST: HUNTING!

YOUR MAJESTY! WE ADVISE AGAINST IT!

I'M NOT A BOY ANY MORE!

ISN'T THAT HOW YOU DIED? I HEARD YOU BROKE YOUR LEG HUNTING AND IT GOT INFECTED.

IN FACT, YOU DIED SO YOUNG, THEY DIDN'T HAVE A PYRAMID READY, SO THEY PUT YOU IN A TEENY-WEENY TOMB.

THEY WHAT!? IT'S AN OUTRAGE! IT'S UNFAIR! I WANT MY MUMMM!

TUT TUT! DON'T BUST YOUR BANDAGES!

HOKUSAI

THIS WEEK, I'M **THRILLED** TO HAVE ONE OF MY **PERSONAL HEROES** ON THE SHOW. IT'S MASTER OF A **MILLION** DRAWINGS, KATSUSHIKA HOKUSAI!

KONNICHIWA!

HOKUSAI, YOU PRODUCED A STAGGERING **35 THOUSAND** DRAWINGS AND PAINTINGS IN YOUR LIFETIME. THAT'S MORE THAN ONE **EVERY SINGLE DAY!**

HEE HEE! WHAT CAN I SAY? I **REALLY** LOVED DRAWING!

SO MUCH SO, THAT I EVEN CHANGED MY NAME, TO **GAKYŌ RŌJIN MANJI**, WHICH MEANS "THE OLD MAN MAD ABOUT DRAWING."

HEH! PEOPLE ACTUALLY HAD TO CALL ME THAT!

MORNING, OLD-MAN-MAD-ABOUT-DRAWING!

HEY! OLD-MAN-MAD-ABOUT-DRAWING! LOVE YOUR WORK!

OLD-MAN-MAD-ABOUT-DRAWING! DINNER'S READY!

THAT'S **CRAZY!** AND SOME OF YOUR **PAINTINGS** WERE PRETTY CRAZY TOO!

HEE HEE! LIKE WHEN I WAS SUMMONED TO COMPETE FOR THE SHOGUN.*

P'KAW! P'KAW!

CHASE! CHASE!

DIP!

* MILITARY RULER OF JAPAN

"RED MAPLE LEAVES FLOATING IN THE RIVER"!

CLAP! CLAP!

YOU BECAME THE MOST POPULAR ARTIST IN JAPAN!

SURE, I GUESS, BUT THAT STUFF REALLY ISN'T IMPORTANT...

WHAT I **REALLY** WANTED WAS TO UNDERSTAND THE NATURE OF THE **WORLD**.

THROUGH UNDERSTANDING THEIR SHAPES, I SOUGHT TO UNDERSTAND THE ESSENCE OF ALL THINGS.

BUT HONESTLY, EVERYTHING I DID BEFORE THE AGE OF **SEVENTY** WAS NOT WORTH BOTHERING ABOUT.

ARE YOU **KIDDING!** I WOULD **KILL** TO BE ABLE TO DRAW LIKE THAT!

CALM DOWN! YOU JUST NEED TO KEEP PRACTISING AND NOT GIVE UP!

I WAS ALREADY AN OLD MAN BY THE TIME I STARTED TO **REALLY** GET IT...

YOU KNOW... THAT'S NOT BAD...

BUT, ALAS, LIFE IS SHORT...

JUST FIVE MORE YEARS...

AND I COULD'VE BEEN...

A **REAL** ARTIST.

SIGH...

IF ONLY I'D HAD MORE **TIME**...

WELL, I THINK IT'S AN ABSOLUTE **INSPIRATION!**

MORE TIME...

I MEAN, YOU ALWAYS KEPT STRIVING, NEVER GETTING DISCOURAGED AND...

HEY!

WAIT! COME BACK! YOU NEED TO GO BACK IN THE GROUND!

JUST A FEW MORE DRAWINGS... I'VE ALMOST GOT IT!

A Brush with Greatness

Hokusai was always a great showman. Another of his many publicity stunts was a **300-foot-long** portrait of the Buddhist saint **Daruma**, which he drew for the Tokyo Festival in 1817.

It was **so big** he had to keep his ink in a bucket, and paint with a broom!

MARIE ANTOINETTE

MY GUEST THIS WEEK PLUNGED HEAD-FIRST FROM RICHES TO RAGS! IT'S THE LAST QUEEN OF FRANCE, MARIE ANTOINETTE!

ENCHANTÉ.

MARIE, YOU LIVED IN LUXURY WHILE YOUR PEOPLE STARVED. WHEN YOU HEARD THAT THEY COULDN'T AFFORD BREAD, YOU FAMOUSLY SAID "LET THEM EAT CAKE!"

THAT'S PRETTY COLD!

VILE SLANDER! TOTALLY NOT TRUE!

BUT IT'S ONE OF THE MOST FAMOUS THINGS ABOUT YOU...

UGH! I CAN'T BELIEVE PEOPLE ARE STILL TELLING LIES ABOUT ME!

THE SAME THING HAPPENED AT COURT! THE PEOPLE WERE ALWAYS POLITE TO MY FACE, BUT BEHIND MY BACK THEY SPREAD THE MOST HORRIBLE GOSSIP!

WELL, I HEARD THAT SHE...

WHISPER WHISPER

PST PST

YOU DON'T SAY!

I'M SURE THEY WERE JUST JEALOUS!

I'M SURE THEY WERE, BUT IT STILL HURT!

MY HUSBAND, THE KING, WASN'T MUCH HELP. HE WAS MORE INTERESTED IN HIS LOCKS...

NOT NOW, DEAR...

WEIRD HOBBY...

YOU MUST'VE BEEN REALLY LONELY.

I KNOW. I KEPT MYSELF DISTRACTED.

...I HELD LATE NIGHT GAMBLING PARTIES...

MASKED BALLS AT THE PALACE OF VERSAILLES...

...AND THE MOST BEAUTIFUL DRESSES...

BUT, ALL THIS WAS WHILE PEOPLE WERE STARVING!

OH, COME ON! I WAS JUST A TEENAGER! I GOT MARRIED AT FOURTEEN!

DON'T TELL ME YOU NEVER DID ANYTHING STUPID AS A TEENAGER!

AH... OK... FAIR POINT.

AND, AS I GOT OLDER, I TRIED TO HELP IN MY OWN WAY. I SPENT LESS, AND GAVE WHAT WE SAVED TO THE POOR...

BUT IT WAS TOO LATE. THE PEOPLE HAD ALREADY MADE UP THEIR MIND ABOUT ME.

SO WHEN THE FRENCH REVOLUTION HAPPENED, YOU WERE IN REAL TROUBLE!

ZUT ALORS! TELL ME ABOUT IT!

THE PEOPLE DIDN'T WANT A KING AND QUEEN ANY MORE SO THEY KICKED US OFF THE THRONE, AND I BECAME THE TARGET OF THEIR HATRED!

THEY STORMED VERSAILLES! I NARROWLY ESCAPED A CROWD OF ANGRY WOMEN WITH KNIVES!

WE HATCHED AN ESCAPE PLAN. DISGUISED AS PEASANTS WE ESCAPED INTO THE NIGHT...

BUT WE WERE DISCOVERED! THANK YOU, MY GOOD MAN...

THEY BROUGHT US BACK, AND SENTENCED US TO... THE GUILLOTINE!

AND, WELL, YOU KNOW WHAT HAPPENED NEXT...

YOU REMAINED VERY CALM. IN FACT, YOU COULD SAY YOU KEPT YOUR HEAD!

FUNNY. I'M LAUGHING MY HEAD OFF.

THIS WEEK, MY GUEST IS THE MAN WHOSE NAME HAS GONE DOWN IN **LEGEND** AS THE **EPITOME** OF THE DASHING, DARING, GALLANT HIGHWAYMAN— DICK TURPIN!

DICK, THERE WAS A TIME WHEN ALL ENGLAND **TREMBLED** AT THE VERY **THOUGHT** OF HEARING THOSE TERRIBLE WORDS...

"STAND AND DELIVER! YOUR MONEY OR YOUR LIFE!"

YEP, QUITE A HERO! MUST BE QUITE A **THRILL** TO MEET ME!

UM, HATE TO PULL YOU OFF YOUR **HIGH HORSE**...

BUT I DID SAY THAT WAS THE **LEGEND**. HERE ON CORPSE TALK, WE ONLY WANT THE **REAL STORY**!

THE... UH... THE **REAL STORY**...?

YEAH, THE **REAL** STORY! WHERE YOU'RE ACTUALLY A LYING, COWARDLY, GOOD-FOR-NOTHING **MEANIE**!

BY GEORGE! NO MAN INSULTS DICK TURPIN AND LIVES!

FFFF

BLAST! POWDER MUST BE DAMP...

YEAH, THAT'LL HAPPEN WHEN YOU'RE SIX FEET UNDERGROUND...

SHALL WE CONTINUE...?

YOU GOT YOUR START WITH THE **ESSEX GANG**...

WANTED

FOR SHEEP-STEALING, HOUSE-BREAKING AND NOSE-PICKING

DASHING, FEARLESS...

YOUR SPECIALTY WAS ROBBING OLD LADIES...

OH, YOU KNOW ABOUT THAT...

I KNOW ABOUT **EVERYTHING**, DICK...

YOU ONCE TURNED AN OLD LADY OVER THE FIRE TO MAKE HER TELL YOU WHERE SHE HID HER LIFE SAVINGS.

NOT VERY HEROIC.

OK, TRUE. BUT AFTER THEY ALL GOT ARRESTED, I TEAMED UP WITH **TOM KING**, THE **GENTLEMAN HIGHWAYMAN**...

TOM WAS FAMOUS FOR HIS **CHIVALRY**. HE WOULDN'T STEAL FROM **LADIES**...

WELL... OK. ONCE HE'D GONE I WENT BACK AND ROBBED THEM ANYWAY...

AND THEN THERE WAS THE **RESCUE ATTEMPT**...

AW! DO WE **HAVE** TO TELL THAT STORY?

TOM GOT ARRESTED, SO I RODE IN TO THE RESCUE!

POW! POW!

BUT...

ARGH! CALL THIS A RESCUE MISSION?! YOU'VE SHOT **ME**!

IT'S TRUE! IT'S TRUE!

I'M A **FAILURE**!

ALL RIGHT, COME ON. IT'S NOT **THAT** BAD. LOTS OF PEOPLE MADE A WORSE HASH OF IT THAN YOU...

AND YOU WERE KINDA BRAVE AT THE END, AFTER YOU GOT CAUGHT AND SENTENCED TO HANG...

WOOP! TIME'S UP! I GUESS WE'LL LEAVE THIS STORY **DANGLING**...

HONK!

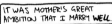

Duvet Days

After returning home from the Crimea, Florence Nightingale proceeded to spend the rest of her life, over 40 years, in bed. (It is now thought that she may have contracted an illness that made her tired all the time.)

Despite this, she still managed to keep up an enormous correspondence, writing over 14,000 (extremely long) letters. That's one a day, every day for the rest of her life!

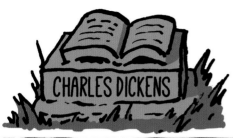

THIS WEEK, MY GUEST IS THE MAN VOTED AS "HISTORY'S GREATEST BRITON"! IT'S THE **BRITISH BULLDOG, SIR WINSTON CHURCHILL**!

SIR WINSTON, YOUR **FIGHTING SPIRIT** BROUGHT BRITAIN THROUGH THE DARK DAYS OF **WORLD WAR TWO**. BUT THAT WASN'T YOUR FIRST BATTLE, WAS IT?

FAR FROM IT! FROM WHEN I WAS REALLY YOUNG, I LOVED NOTHING BETTER THAN PLAYING WITH MY TOY SOLDIERS.

AND IT WASN'T LONG BEFORE THE WAR GAMES BECAME REALITY, FIRST AS A CAVALRY OFFICER, AND THEN AS A WAR REPORTER!

I HAD SOME DASHED GOOD ADVENTURES DOING WAR REPORTING! LIKE ONE TIME IN SOUTH AFRICA...

OUR TRAIN WAS ATTACKED, SO I CARRIED THE WOUNDED TO SAFETY AND GOT THE ENGINE RUNNING AGAIN.

STAY COOL, CHAPS! THIS WILL BE GOOD MATERIAL FOR MY PAPER!

I WAS CAPTURED, BUT I ESCAPED AND CAME BACK TO ENGLAND A HERO!

YOUR HERO STATUS LAUNCHED YOU INTO A SUCCESSFUL CAREER IN POLITICS!

HMPH! NOT SO SUCCESSFUL!

I MADE A **LOT** OF MISTAKES, LOST ELECTIONS, CHANGED PARTY **TWICE**, AND WAS **EXCLUDED** BY MY OWN GOVERNMENT!

AND MY OWN DARK MOODS FOLLOWED ME AROUND. I CALLED THEM MY **BLACK DOGS**.

WINSTON...

YOU SUCK...

BUT AS I ALWAYS SAID: IF YOU'RE GOING THROUGH HELL, **KEEP GOING**! AND THOSE WERE HELLISH TIMES INDEED...

HITLER HAD TURNED GERMANY INTO A NAZI WAR-MACHINE, AND NOW HE WAS READY TO TAKE OVER THE WORLD...

NEVILLE CHAMBERLAIN, THE PRIME MINISTER, ARGUED THAT GERMANY WAS TOO STRONG, SO WE SHOULD **SURRENDER**.

BUT I SAID **NO**! WE WILL **NEVER GIVE UP**!

SO THEY GAVE NEVILLE THE BOOT AND MADE **YOU** P.M. INSTEAD.

FOR A LONG TIME, IT LOOKED AS THOUGH BRITAIN WOULD **LOSE** THE WAR! RATIONING, AIR RAIDS AND MILITARY DEFEATS HAD MORALE AT AN ALL-TIME LOW...

BUT YOUR ROUSING SPEECHES REMINDED THEM WHAT THEY WERE FIGHTING FOR...

WE SHALL FIGHT THEM ON THE BEACHES...

WE SHALL FIGHT THEM IN THE FIELDS AND IN THE STREETS! WE SHALL **NEVER SURRENDER**!

AND YOU NEVER DID. YOU STAYED WORKING IN LONDON, EVEN DURING THE WORST OF THE **BLITZ**.

BOOM BOOM!

YOU WORKED FEROCIOUSLY UNTIL THE WAR WAS WON, STAYING UP UNTIL 4.30am MOST NIGHTS!

HOW DID YOU MANAGE IT? AH! I HAD A **SECRET TECHNIQUE**!

I HAD A **BED** IN MY OFFICE AND EVERY AFTERNOON I'D PUT IN **EARPLUGS** (IN CASE OF AIR-RAID) AND HAVE A LITTLE SLEEP!

I CALLED IT A **POWER NAP**!

THERE YOU HAVE IT, FOLKS. HOW WE WON THE WAR: COURAGE, GRIT AND FREQUENT NAPS.

Z...

The Music Thief

Mozart's ability to hear and memorise music in his head was legendary. When he was 14, he visited the **Vatican** to hear a famous piece of music, the Miserere by Allegri. It was an amazingly complex piece, featuring not one, but **two choirs** singing at the same time.

The Vatican guarded it closely, keeping the written music locked up so that no one else could play it. But Mozart listened to it once, then walked out and wrote down the **whole thing** from memory!

THIS WEEK, MY GUEST IS THE WOMAN WHO GAVE BIRTH TO A **MODERN MONSTER**! IT'S THE **GRANDMASTER OF GOTHIC**, FRANKENSTEIN CREATOR **MARY SHELLEY**!

HELLO EVERYONE!

OH GEEZ, YOU'RE NOT GOING TO TO TALK LIKE THAT THE WHOLE TIME?!

SORRY.

MARY, YOUR WHOLE **LIFE** READS LIKE SOME STRANGE GOTHIC FAIRY TALE...

YOU EVEN HAD A **WICKED STEPMOTHER** WHO MADE YOU DO THE HOUSEHOLD CHORES...

JUST LIKE **CINDERELLA**!

I KNOW!

BUT THEN YOU MET YOUR **PRINCE CHARMING**...

PERCY SHELLEY WAS A POET-PHILOSOPHER. OH, HE WAS **BRILLIANT**! WE WENT FOR WALKS BY MY DEAR MOTHER'S GRAVE, AND FELL IN LOVE...

SO DREAMY...

ONLY ONE PROBLEM, HE WAS ALREADY MARRIED!

FATHER FORBADE US FROM SEEING EACH OTHER, SO WE RAN AWAY!

WE TOURED EUROPE, TRYING TO OUTRUN THE SCANDAL. BUT WE COULDN'T OUTRUN **TRAGEDY**...

OUR FIRST CHILD DIED WHEN HE WAS ONLY ONE YEAR OLD...

PERCY TRIED TO CHEER ME UP WITH A HOLIDAY WITH OUR FRIENDS ON LAKE GENEVA.

IT'S NOT VERY **CHEERY**...

IT'S **GREAT**! YOU'LL LOVE IT!

WE WERE ALL SITTING AROUND THE FIRE ONE EVENING, READING GHOST STORIES...

WHEN PERCY'S FRIEND **LORD BYRON** HAD AN IDEA.

I SAY! LET'S ALL WRITE ONE OF OUR OWN!

THE OTHERS ALL STARTED THEIRS (AND THEN GAVE UP) BUT I JUST **COULDN'T** THINK OF AN IDEA!

THEY KEPT TEASING ME: "HOW'S YOUR **GHOST STORY** COMING ALONG...?"

BUT THEN, ONE DAY, I HEARD THEM TALKING ABOUT A NEW SCIENTIFIC DISCOVERY, CALLED **GALVANISH**.

SCIENTISTS HAD FOUND A WAY TO MAKE DEAD ANIMALS MOVE BY APPLYING A JOLT OF ELECTRICITY TO THEIR CORPSES.

SUDDENLY, I SAW IT ALL...

I SAW THE PALE **DOCTOR FRANKENSTEIN**, KNEELING BESIDE THE **THING** THAT HE HAD CREATED...

I FELT HIS TERROR AS HE GAVE THE **SPARK OF LIFE** TO A **HIDEOUS CORPSE**!

YOUR **TALE OF TERROR** CONTINUES TO SCARE THE **PANTS** OFF PEOPLE, EVEN CENTURIES LATER!

BUT IT ALSO HAS A **SERIOUS MESSAGE**...!

DON'T MESS AROUND WITH CORPSES!

RIGHT!

UNLESS YOU'RE A **TRAINED PROFESSIONAL** LIKE ME!

UH...

CLEOPATRA

This week, my guest is the woman who **stole the hearts** of Rome's greatest leaders. History's **most evil woman**, or a **brilliant survivor** in a difficult time? **You decide!** It's the last pharaoh of Egypt, queen of the Nile, **CLEOPATRA!**

CLEO, YOU SHARED THE RULE OF EGYPT WITH YOUR LITTLE BROTHER (AND HUSBAND) PTOLEMY XIII. ONLY ONE PROBLEM...

YOU DIDN'T LIKE TO SHARE!

I'D ALREADY BEEN **BANISHED** FOR TRYING TO TAKE THE THRONE FOR MYSELF. I NEEDED **HELP**, AND ONLY **ONE MAN** WAS POWERFUL ENOUGH FOR THE JOB...

JULIUS CAESAR! BUT WITH MY BROTHER HUNTING FOR ME, I HAD TO BE **CUNNING**...

KEEP AN EYE OUT FOR CLEOPATRA!

NO WAY SHE'S GETTING IN HERE!

A NEW CARPET FOR CAESAR?!

RIGHT THIS WAY!

? !

HE FELL HEAD OVER HEELS IN LOVE WITH YOU, AND MADE YOU THE MOST POWERFUL WOMAN IN THE WORLD!

JUST TO MAKE SURE, YOU HAD YOUR BROTHER AND ALL YOUR OTHER SIBLINGS **KILLED!** THAT'S PRETTY RUTHLESS.

AW! THANKS!

YOU WERE ON TOP OF THE WORLD, BUT THEN... CAESAR WAS **MURDERED!***

WHA?!

* SEE PAGE 35

YOU NEEDED ANOTHER ROMAN PROTECTOR, AND **FAST!** YOU HOOKED CAESAR'S NUMBER 2, **MARK ANTONY.**

NOW HERE'S ONE THING I DON'T UNDERSTAND. HOW'D YOU MANAGE TO SEDUCE ALL THESE ROMANS WHEN YOU WERE, ACCORDING TO ONE HISTORIAN, "NOT THAT HOT"?

WHAT?! WHO SAYS THAT?! I'LL HAVE HIM KILLED! I'LL HAVE HIS FAMILY KILLED! I'LL HAVE EVERYONE WHO EVER **KNEW** HIM KILLED AND MAKE IT ILLEGAL TO SAY HIS NAME!

I CAN DO THAT, YOU KNOW.

UH, WELL... YOU'RE A BIT LATE. HE'S BEEN DEAD FOR CENTURIES.

ANYWAYS, IF YOU WANT TO **CATCH A MAN** IT TAKES MORE THAN LOOKS! I HAD THE **POWER OF PERSONALITY!**

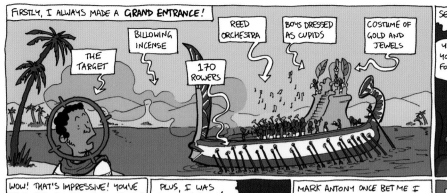

HENRY VIII

THIS WEEK, MY GUEST IS A MAN WITH AN **ENORMOUS** APPETITE FOR LIFE! IT'S THE **KING WITH THE BLING**, THE **TUDOR RUDEBOY**, HENRY VIII!

YEEEAH, CHEKKIT!

HENRY, AS A YOUNG KING, YOU WERE AMAZINGLY POPULAR!

YES! EVERYONE LOVED ME FOR MY GENEROSITY AND RUGGED GOOD LOOKS!

BUT YOU HAD ONE PROBLEM...

NO HEIR. YOUR WIFE HAD MANY CHILDREN, BUT ONLY ONE SURVIVED, A **GIRL**.

WITHOUT A SON, THE **TUDOR DYNASTY** WOULD **DIE OUT!**

I NEEDED A **NEW WIFE**, AND **FAST!**

...AND I ALREADY HAD SOMEONE IN MIND FOR THE JOB...

ANNE BOLEYN! PRETTY, CLEVER, CHARMING; SHE HAD ME IN A WHIRL!

BUT THE CHURCH DIDN'T ALLOW **DIVORCE.** YOU APPLIED TO THE POPE FOR **SPECIAL PERMISSION.**

BUT HE WOULDN'T ALLOW IT!

Dear Pope, please please please

BUT THEN I GOT THINKING... WHY SHOULD THE KING BE TOLD WHAT TO DO BY **ANYONE?!** WASN'T I APPOINTED BY **GOD?!**

WHAT IF I MADE MY **OWN** CHURCH? THEN **I'D** BE IN CHARGE AND I COULD DO WHAT I LIKED!

SO THAT'S JUST WHAT I DID! I GAVE MY WIFE THE BOOT AND MARRIED ANNE INSTEAD.

THE POPE **EXCOMMUNICATED** ME, BUT I DIDN'T CARE. I HAD MY **OWN** CHURCH NOW.

AND THE FUN DIDN'T STOP THERE! I ALSO GOT RID OF ALL THE MONASTERIES AND KICKED OUT THE MONKS.

I **NEEDED** THAT LAND TO BRIBE- I MEAN **REWARD** MY LOYAL SUPPORTERS.

YOU KICKED OUT THE MONKS?! PEOPLE WHO DEVOTED THEIR LIVES TO HELPING OTHERS?!

PFF. **PARASITES!**

OK, SOME PEOPLE GOT MAD.

INDIA WAS PART OF THE BRITISH EMPIRE, AND THE BRITISH HAD ALL SORTS OF WAYS TO GET RICH AT OUR EXPENSE.

HO HO!

MAN...

THAT'S WHEN I STARTED WEARING THE DHOTI.

THE WHAT!?

THIS STYLISH GARMENT. LIKE A BIG NAPPY. INDIANS HAD BEEN WEARING IT FOR CENTURIES.

INSTEAD OF BUYING EXPENSIVE BRITISH CLOTHES, WE COULD MAKE OUR OWN! I ALWAYS LED BY EXAMPLE, SO THAT'S WHAT I DID.'

BUT WEARING NAPPIES WASN'T GOING TO GET THE BRITISH OUT OF INDIA! IT WAS TIME TO BRING OUT THE BIG GUNS...

NON-COOPERATION!

IF A LAW WAS EVIL AND WRONG, WE'D JUST REFUSE TO FOLLOW IT.'

BUT IF YOU BROKE THE LAW, DIDN'T YOU GET PUT IN JAIL?

HEE HEE! ALL THE TIME!

SOON, THERE WERE SO MANY PEOPLE IN JAIL, THEY RAN OUT OF ROOM!

AND OF COURSE, THEY COULD BEAT AND KILL US, BUT LOVE IS STRONGER THAN FEAR!

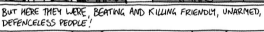

PICTURE IT! THOUSANDS OF PEOPLE ALL LINING UP FEARLESSLY TO BE BEATEN.

HEY! NO PUSHING!

THERE'S ENOUGH FOR EVERYONE!

LADIES FIRST!

OI! WHAT ABOUT ME THEN?!

JUST A MINUTE, MY ARM'S TIRED OUT!

THE WORLD WAS HORRIFIED! BRITAIN WAS HORRIFIED! THEY THOUGHT THEY WERE CIVILISED...

BUT HERE THEY WERE, BEATING AND KILLING FRIENDLY, UNARMED, DEFENCELESS PEOPLE!

I'M EMBARRASSED.

MAKES YOU ASHAMED TO BE BRITISH!

NOT CROQUET, WHAT?

ALTHOUGH IT TOOK ANOTHER TWELVE YEARS, IT WAS AT THAT MOMENT I KNEW THE BRITISH WOULD LEAVE INDIA.

BUT DOES IT REALLY WORK?! EVEN AFTER ALL YOU HAVE TAUGHT, PEOPLE ARE STILL FIGHTING AND KILLING ONE ANOTHER!

YOU WERE SHOT DEAD BY A YOUNG MAN WHO WAS ANGRY THAT YOU DIDN'T HATE MUSLIMS.

WILL LOVE REALLY WIN IN THE END?! WILL WE EVER LEARN TO LIVE IN PEACE?!

WILL WE?! WILL WE REALLY, GANDHI!?!

THERE, THERE.

UH... YOU'RE GETTING MY NAPPY WET...

THIS WEEK, I'M HONOURED TO INTRODUCE THE LADY WHO MAPPED THE DEPTHS OF THE HEART, WITHOUT EVER LEAVING HER FAMILY HOME! IT'S THE **PEERLESS PRINCESS** OF **PERIOD DRAMA**, **JANE AUSTEN!**

HOW PLEASANT.

JANE, YOU'RE NOW A **BILLION DOLLAR** INDUSTRY, SPAWNING COUNTLESS BOOKS, MOVIES AND TV SHOWS.

REALLY? HOW VERY GRATIFYING.

WHILE I WAS ALIVE, I WAS COMPLETELY UNKNOWN! IN FACT, I HAD TO PUBLISH MY BOOKS **ANONYMOUSLY** BECAUSE WRITING NOVELS WASN'T CONSIDERED **LADYLIKE.**

YOUR NOVELS FOLLOW THE TRIALS AND TRIBULATIONS OF FINDING A HUSBAND. AND YET YOU YOURSELF NEVER MARRIED. HOW COULD YOU WRITE ABOUT IT SO WELL?

JUST BECAUSE I NEVER MARRIED DOESN'T MEAN I NEVER FELL IN LOVE! I MET **TOM LEFROY** WHEN I WAS JUST 20...

EVERY SCANDALOUS THING YOU CAN THINK OF, FROM **DANCING** TO **SITTING TOGETHER,** WE DID IT!

YOU THINK **SITTING TOGETHER** IS SCANDALOUS...?

IT WAS IN **MY DAY!**

BUT... UH... **WE'RE** SITTING TOGETHER....!

GASP!

FAINT!

A SHORT WHILE LATER...

DO PRAY EXCUSE ME...

PLEASE, THINK NOTHING OF IT. SHALL WE CONTINUE?

YES, LET'S!

YOU WERE TELLING US ABOUT TOM LEFROY. WHY DIDN'T YOU MARRY HIM?

OH, HIS FAMILY WOULDN'T ALLOW IT.

THEY DECIDED MY FAMILY WAS TOO **POOR,** SO THEY SENT HIM AWAY. I NEVER SAW HIM AGAIN.

HOW AWFUL!

I WAS **HEART BROKEN!** HOW **DARE** THEY DECIDE ON MY FUTURE HAPPINESS LIKE THAT!

I POURED OUT MY SOUL ONTO PAPER, WRITING A NOVEL ABOUT A YOUNG LADY WHO MARRIES THE MAN SHE LOVES, **DESPITE** HIS FAMILY'S OBJECTIONS!

-SNIFF!- IT BECAME YOUR MOST FAMOUS STORY, **PRIDE AND PREJUDICE!**

BUT THEN, HEARTACHE TURNED TO **MISERY** WHEN FATHER RETIRED AND MOVED US TO THAT **FOUL DEN OF LIES**...

BATH!

LOOKS LIKE A JOLLY NICE PLACE TO ME...

NO! IT'S ALL A FAÇADE!

THE HOUSES ARE ALL PRETTY IN THE FRONT AND UGLY BEHIND!

AND THE **PEOPLE** ARE JUST AS BAD — POLITE AND FRIENDLY TO YOUR FACE...

AND **MEAN** AND **RUDE** BEHIND YOUR BACK!

ALSO, THAT'S WHERE EVERYONE WENT TO TRY AND GET MARRIED! TO SEE THEM ALL ACTING **SO** POLITE WHEN REALLY THEY JUST WANTED TO FIND OUT WHO HAD THE MOST MONEY! **SICKENING!**

I COULDN'T GET ANY WRITING DONE THERE. I WAS TOO MISERABLE.

IT WAS DURING THIS TIME THAT YOU RECEIVED YOUR ONLY PROPOSAL OF MARRIAGE.

YEAH. **"ONLY"** PROPOSAL! **ONLY ONE!** WELL, AT LEAST I GOT ONE! SOME PEOPLE DON'T GET **ANY! HUH?! HUH?!**

-AHEM!- EXCUSE ME... I MEAN, YES, THAT'S RIGHT! WE WERE VISITING FRIENDS WHEN THEIR YOUNGEST SON, **HARRIS BIGG-WITHER,** PROPOSED.

HE WAS RICH, AND MY FAMILY WERE QUITE POOR. IT WOULD HAVE ALLOWED ME TO SUPPORT MY PARENTS AND MY SISTER.

BUT THERE WAS A PROBLEM...

WELL, YOU'RE NOT CALLED **JANE BIGG-WITHER** ARE YOU?

HOW DID YOU KNOW?

WELL, YES. THERE WAS **ONE** PROBLEM. HE WAS **LOUD, STUPID** AND **RUDE!** I COULDN'T MARRY A MAN LIKE THAT!

I CALLED IT OFF THE NEXT DAY!

SCANDALOUS!

YES, BUT IN MY NOVELS, THE HEROINE ALWAYS FOLLOWS HER HEART! EVEN WHEN IT'S **DIFFICULT!** EVEN WHEN IT **HURTS!**

I NEVER FOUND A HUSBAND, BUT I FOUND LOVE IN THE STORIES AND CHARACTERS I CREATED.

AND GAVE **MILLIONS** THE PLEASURE OF GETTING **LOST IN AN AUSTEN!**

The Lost Austen

Jane Austen's sister, Cassandra, earned the undying hatred of Austen scholars everywhere by **burning** almost all of Jane's letters. She seems to have been afraid that, if they were made public, they would spoil the Austen family's image of "good quiet Aunt Jane".

We can only **guess** what illicit secrets they contained...

THIS WEEK, MY GUEST IS THE **TALLEST, BEARDIEST** AND **MOST FAMOUS** PRESIDENT OF THE UNITED STATES OF AMERICA! IT'S "HONEST" ABRAHAM LINCOLN!

WHY, HELLO, YOUNG FELLER!

ABE, YOU'RE KNOWN AS "THE GREAT EMANCIPATOR" FOR YOUR ROLE IN FREEING AMERICA'S SLAVES...

HONESTLY, THAT WAS AN **ACCIDENT.** I ALWAYS THOUGHT THAT SLAVERY WAS WRONG, BUT I NEVER THOUGHT I'D BE ABLE TO PUT AN END TO IT.

NOW, AT THIS TIME, THERE WERE SOME STATES WHERE PEOPLE COULD KEEP SLAVES, AND SOME STATES WHERE THEY COULDN'T...

FREEMEN

SLAVES

WHEN I WAS ELECTED PRESIDENT, SOME FOLKS BECAME CONVINCED I WOULD FORCE THEM TO GIVE UP THEIR SLAVES.

IT AIN'T RIGHT!

IT'S UNJUST!

HE'S GONNA TAKE AWAY OUR BASIC RIGHTS!

SPEAKIN' OF BEING ELECTED, THAT REMINDS ME OF A FUNNY STORY. DO YOU KNOW WHY I HAVE THIS **BEARD?**

UH...

I GOT A LETTER FROM A LITTLE GIRL WHO THOUGHT I WOULD STAND A BETTER CHANCE OF BEING ELECTED WITH A BEARD.

SO I GREW ONE, AND BY GOLLY, I GOT ELECTED!

HOW ABOUT THAT? SO, UH...THE STATES THAT WANTED TO SPLIT OFF...?

WELL, I SURE AS SHOOTIN' WASN'T GOING TO STAND FOR **THAT!** THE UNITED STATES WAS MEANT TO BE **UNITED,** AND I INTENDED TO KEEP IT THAT WAY!

THIS WAS THE START OF THE **AMERICAN CIVIL WAR!**

AND IT WAS THE WAR THAT LED TO YOU FREEING THE SLAVES...?

WELL, HERE WAS THE WAY OF IT...

AT FIRST, I **COULDN'T** FREE THEM, AS I DIDN'T WANT TO LOSE THE FEW SLAVE STATES THAT WERE STILL ON OUR SIDE.

NOW, NOW BOYS...

BUT THE WAR DRAGGED ON AND ON. **SO** MANY MEN HAD BEEN KILLED, IT BECAME A QUESTION OF WHICH SIDE HAD THE MOST MEN LEFT!

IF WE RECRUITED BLACK SOLDIERS, WE'D HAVE ENOUGH MEN TO WIN THE WAR!

WELL, YOU CAN'T ASK A MAN TO FIGHT FOR HIS FREEDOM AND THEN MAKE HIM GO BACK TO BEING A SLAVE, NOW CAN YOU?!

SO ON NEW YEAR'S DAY, 1863, I SIGNED THE MOST IMPORTANT DOCUMENT OF MY LIFE: **THE EMANCIPATION PROCLAMATION!**

MR. PRESIDENT... WHERE IS IT?

OH, ABE!

WHAT A HOOT!

YOU JOKER!

THAT'S ONE THING PEOPLE MIGHT NOT KNOW ABOUT YOU – YOU LOVED TO TELL JOKES AND FUNNY STORIES...

HEH! WELL, WITH ALL THE PRESSURE I WAS UNDER, IF I DIDN'T I'D GO MAD!

THAT REMINDS ME OF ONE TIME I WAS IN THE BACK-WOODS WHEN A MAN CAME UP TO ME WITH A RIFLE!

WHOA NOW! WHAT'S THIS, FRIEND?

I MADE A VOW: IF I EVER SAW AN **UGLIER** MAN THAN ME, I'D **SHOOT** HIM!

WELL, IN THAT CASE, THEN **SHOOT!** IF I'M UGLIER'N YOU, I **DON'T** WANT TO LIVE!

HAR HAR! IN THAT CASE THEN SHOOT! OH, I CRACK ME UP!

THIS WEEK, MY GUEST IS THE MAN WHOSE THOUGHTS TRAVEL AT **THE SPEED OF LIGHT!** IT'S THE GENIUS WHO REWROTE THE LAWS OF SPACE AND TIME, **ALBERT EINSTEIN!**

BLAAA!

DUDE! DO YOU MIND?

ALBERT EINSTEIN

EINSTEIN, EVERYONE KNOWS YOU'RE AN INCREDIBLE GENIUS. BUT YOU WERE A TERRIBLE STUDENT AND YOU HATED SCHOOL. HOW IS THAT POSSIBLE?

IT WAS, I THINK, NOT ONLY POSSIBLE BUT **NECESSARY!** I WAS SO CURIOUS TO UNDERSTAND THE WORLD, BUT SCHOOL SOUGHT ONLY TO **DRILL ME TO MEMORISE MEANINGLESS FACTS.**

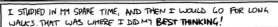

BUT **ALL** MY GREAT DISCOVERIES CAME, NOT FROM FOLLOWING BLINDLY, BUT FROM WONDER, CURIOSITY AND ALLOWING MYSELF TO THINK DIFFERENTLY.

YOU WERE TRYING TO SOLVE SOME OF THE GREATEST PUZZLES OF SCIENCE, WHICH HAD ELUDED SCIENTISTS FOR CENTURIES!

I STUDIED IN MY SPARE TIME, AND THEN I WOULD GO FOR LONG WALKS. THAT WAS WHERE I DID MY **BEST THINKING!**

YOUR NEW THEORIES TURNED OUR UNDERSTANDING OF THE WORLD **UPSIDE DOWN!** CAN YOU EXPLAIN THEM TO US?

PEOPLE WERE **ALWAYS** ASKING ME THAT! I BECAME SO FAMOUS I COULDN'T WALK IN THE STREET WITHOUT **SOMEONE** STOPPING ME TO EXPLAIN MY THEORIES!

SO I DEVELOPED AN **ESCAPE PLAN...**

SO SORRY. WRONG GUY! PEOPLE ARE **ALWAYS** MISTAKING ME FOR THIS GUY EINSTEIN...

BUT I **KNOW** YOU'RE EINSTEIN! YOU CAN'T GET OUT OF IT THAT WAY!

OK, OK. BUT I CAN'T EXPLAIN THE **WHOLE THING.** WE ONLY HAVE TWO PAGES!

WELL, EVERYONE'S HEARD OF YOUR MOST FAMOUS EQUATION: $E=MC^2$! CAN YOU EXPLAIN **THAT?**

OK, SURE. THE E IS **ENERGY**, WHICH COULD BE LIGHT OR HEAT OR MOVEMENT - THINGS LIKE THAT.

THE M IS **MASS** - WHICH IS SORT OF LIKE WEIGHT OR SOLID-NESS.

THE = WAS MY BIG DISCOVERY! BEFORE, SCIENTISTS THOUGHT THAT MASS AND ENERGY WERE DIFFERENT THINGS, BUT I REALISED THAT THEY ARE REALLY JUST TWO FORMS OF THE **SAME THING!**

AND THE C^2?

THAT'S THE SPEED OF LIGHT, MULTIPLIED BY ITSELF. BASICALLY, IT'S JUST A **REALLY, REALLY BIG NUMBER!**

BLACK BEARD

MY GUEST THIS WEEK IS THE **TERROR** OF THE HIGH SEAS, THE **SCOURGE** OF THE SPANISH MAIN, THE **CURSE** OF THE CARIBBEAN! IT'S CAPTAIN EDWARD TEACH, BETTER KNOWN AS **BLACKBEARD**!

BLAST YER **BARNACLES**, YE SWABS!

BLACKBEARD! A NAME DESIGNED TO STRIKE FEAR INTO THE STOUTEST OF HEARTS! AND THE NAME WAS JUST THE **FIRST STEP** IN A CALCULATED CAMPAIGN OF **TERROR**...

ARR! WE WOULD ATTACK AT **DUSK** FOR MAXIMUM SNEAKABILITY...

AT FIRST, WE'D FLY THE SAME FLAG AS OUR PREY, TO TRICK THEM INTO THINKING WE WERE FRIENDS...

HEE HEE!

SHH!

THEN, AT THE LAST MINUTE, WE'D HOIST THE **BLACKBEARD JOLLY ROGER**!

HAR! FOOLED YOU!

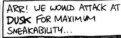

IT'S A SKELETON **TOASTING THE DEVIL** WHILE STABBING A **BLEEDING HEART**. PRETTY BAD-ASS, EH?

THEN, FOR THE BOARDING PARTY, I'D **BRAID** MY BEARD, DRESS ALL IN **BLACK** AND PUT **LIT FUSES** IN MY HAIR, SO I LOOKED LIKE THE **DEVIL HIMSELF**! PEOPLE WERE SO **TERRIFIED**, THEY'D SURRENDER WITHOUT A FIGHT!

AND IF THEY DIDN'T SURRENDER?

THEY **ALWAYS** SURRENDERED.

MY REPUTATION AS A BLOOD-THIRSTY PIRATE WAS SO FEARSOME, I HARDLY EVER HAD TO KILL **ANYONE**!

IN FACT, YOU ACTUALLY WENT OUT OF YOUR WAY TO **NOT** KILL PEOPLE. LIKE THAT TIME IN CHARLESTON...

ARR! CHARLESTON... JEWEL OF THE CAROLINAS! WE DREW ANCHOR JUST OUTSIDE THE HARBOUR, AND FOR A WEEK WE SEIZED ANY SHIP THAT TRIED TO SAIL IN OR OUT, AND TOOK THEM HOSTAGE!

YOU SEE, WE NEEDED MEDICINE...

MEDICINE?

ARR. PIRATES GET SICK TOO...

I DISPATCHED ONE OF THE PRISONERS WITH TWO PIRATES TO BRING BACK MEDICINES. IF THEY WEREN'T BACK IN TWO DAYS, I'D **HANG THE LOT**!

BUT TWO DAYS CAME AND WENT WITH NO SIGN OF THEM...

CAP'N, THE DEADLINE'S PAST. WE'LL LOOK LIKE **WIMPS** IF WE DON'T...

JUST A LITTLE LONGER...

Dreaded, Deaded, Decapitated and Dunked!

Despite having his throat slit, Blackbeard kept on fighting, taking 5 bullets and 20 sword cuts before he fell. After his death his head was cut off and hung from the bowsprit, while his body was thrown into the water.

According to legend, his head then shouted out, "Come on, Edward!" while his body continued to swim around the ship, trying to get back on board to get the head back, before finally sinking. Supposedly, on a moonless night, you can sometimes see the eerie green glow of Blackbeard's headless ghost, still swimming around searching for his head.

Here on Corpse Talk we're usually pretty dubious about legends that obviously didn't happen, but come on – that is just cool.

RICHARD THE LIONHEART

THIS WEEK, MY GUEST IS ONE OF ENGLAND'S MOST BELOVED MONARCHS. IT'S **KING RICHARD THE LIONHEART**! TO THIS DAY, HIS NAME IS A **WATCHWORD** FOR COURAGE, HONOUR AND CHIVALRY...

YEAH!

WHICH IS IRONIC, BECAUSE HE'S ACTUALLY AS BIG A BULLY, SNEAK AND SPOILED BRAT AS YOU COULD EVER WISH **NOT** TO MEET!

WHA?!

BUT... BUT... I AM THE GREAT HERO - KING OF ENGLAND!

WELL, LET'S LOOK AT THE **FACTS** SHALL WE?

YOU WERE HARDLY EVER EVEN **IN** ENGLAND, PREFERRING TO LIVE IN YOUR LANDS IN FRANCE.

WELL, COME ON! ENGLAND IS A **DUMP**! ALWAYS COLD AND RAINING!

YOU BECAME ONE OF THE GREATEST WARRIORS OF ALL TIME...

YEAH! THAT'S MORE LIKE IT!

IN PARTICULAR, YOU BECAME THE MASTER OF USING **SEIGE ENGINES** TO DESTROY THE CASTLES OF YOUR ENEMIES.

ESPECIALLY WHEN THE ENEMY WAS **YOUR OWN FATHER**!

WHAT THE HELL, SON?

DAD, YOU'RE GOING **DOWN**.

AND HE DID. HE DIED OF **STRESS**, CAUSED BY **YOU**!

HEY! HE WANTED ME TO SHARE THE KINGDOM WITH MY LITTLE BROTHER, JOHN. NO **WAY**!

WAH! DON'T WANNA! MINE!

THEN, AS SOON AS YOU BECAME KING, YOU LEFT TO JOIN THE **THIRD CRUSADE**. WHAT WAS **THAT** ALL ABOUT?

THE CRUSADER KINGDOM IN JERUSALEM HAD BEEN CONQUERED BY THE MUSLIMS. I WAS DETERMINED TO TAKE IT BACK!

SO I....

WAIT. WAIT... **WHY**? YOU HAD YOUR OWN KINGDOM. WHY BOTHER WITH WHAT HAPPENED HALF-WAY AROUND THE WORLD?

WELL, LOOK. I'D JUST KILLED MY OWN **DAD**, SO I WAS PRETTY SURE I WAS GOING TO **HELL**. ANYONE WHO TOOK PART IN THE CRUSADES WAS GIVEN A **GUARANTEED** TICKET **STRAIGHT TO HEAVEN**!

SO YOU PLANNED TO GET TO HEAVEN BY KILLING **MORE PEOPLE**? GENIUS.

HEY, IT'S NOT LIKE I WAS ABOUT TO START **DOING GOOD** OR SOMETHING...

ANYWAY, AS I WAS SAYING, I WENT TO JERUSALEM, LEAVING A TRAIL OF TERROR AND DESTRUCTION IN MY WAKE...

TELL US ABOUT THE FALCON.

THE UH... OH...

DO I HAVE TO?

I WAS OUT RIDING ONE DAY WHEN I SAW A PARTICULARLY FINE FALCON IN A POOR MAN'S HUT.

THAT'S **MUCH** TOO FINE A BIRD TO BELONG TO A MERE **PEASANT**...

REALLY, IT'S MY **DUTY**, AS A KING, TO **STEAL** IT...

WHACK!

YOU WERE SET UPON, BEATEN AND KICKED OUT OF THE VILLAGE BY A CROWD OF ANGRY PEASANTS!

ALL RIGHT, ALL RIGHT. LET'S GET ON TO MY GLORIOUS VICTORIES SHALL WE?

YOU MEAN LIKE WHEN YOU RECONQUERED JERUSALEM. OH, WAIT. THAT'S RIGHT. YOU **DIDN'T**!

OKAY, SERIOUSLY, CAN I GET ANOTHER INTERVIEWER?

YOU QUARRELLED WITH YOUR ALLIES, SO THEY ALL LEFT, TAKING THEIR ARMIES WITH THEM.

THEY WERE ALL **IDIOTS**! THEY DIDN'T UNDERSTAND MILITARY STRATEGY!

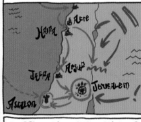

WE HAD JUST ONE CITY. WE NEEDED TO BUILD MORE CASTLES AND BE READY FOR A LONG WAR, BUT THEY JUST WANTED TO ATTACK JERUSALEM AND GO HOME.

PLUS, I HEARD MY LITTLE BROTHER JOHN WAS PLOTTING TO TAKE OVER MY KINGDOM.

SO YOU GAVE UP.

I MADE A **TACTICAL WITHDRAWAL**!

TO GET HOME, I HAD TO PASS THROUGH THE LANDS OF MY ENEMIES, SO I DISGUISED MYSELF AS A **RETURNING PILGRIM**.

SO... HOW DO I LOOK?

VERY GOOD, SIRE.

PEASANTY.

BUT THEY SAW THROUGH YOUR DISGUISE BECAUSE YOU INSISTED ON EATING EXPENSIVE FOODS!

WHAT WAS IT AGAIN?

... ROAST CHICKEN...

.. IT'S MY FAVOURITE.

YOU WERE IMPRISONED, AND YOUR SUBJECTS HAD TO PAY A **KING'S RANSOM** TO GET YOU OUT!

YOUR BROTHER JOHN TRIED TO PAY THEM TO **KEEP** YOU IN PRISON!

BUT BEFORE LONG, YOU WERE BACK HOME, AND BACK TO YOUR OLD WAYS, BEATING AND CHEATING ANYONE WHO EVEN LOOKED AT YOU FUNNY!

OKAY, YOU KNOW WHAT? I'M OUTTA HERE.

ANNE, WHY ON EARTH ARE **YOU** MAD WITH CATHERINE? AFTER ALL, **YOU'RE** THE ONE WHO STOLE **HER** HUSBAND!

SHE COULD'VE JUST GIVEN HIM A DIVORCE. SHE WAS TOO OLD TO HAVE MORE KIDS ANYWAY! BUT SHE HAD TO BE ALL "OOH, HE'S **MY** HUSBAND!"

HENRY **LOVED ME!** HE WROTE ME LOVE LETTERS ALL THE TIME. AND HE **HATED** WRITING!

THAT'S TRUE.

HE DID HATE WRITING.

WHO WOULDN'T?

BUT ALL HIS LOVE TURNED TO **HATE** WHEN YOU GAVE HIM, NOT A MALE HEIR, BUT A **GIRL!**

YEAH ANNE. SERIOUSLY.

IF YOU'D JUST AGREED TO THE DIVORCE I'D HAVE HAD **TIME** TO PRODUCE AN HEIR!

WITCH!

HOME WRECKER!

HAG!

ETC...

SIGH...

AND HENRY MIGHT ALSO HAVE BEEN GROWING TIRED OF YOUR INCREASINGLY VIOLENT TEMPER...

VIOLENT?! WHO SAYS I'M VIOLENT? I'LL KICK THEIR PANTS!

BUT HE'D JUST TURNED THE COUNTRY, AND THE CHURCH, UPSIDE DOWN TO MARRY **YOU!** HE COULDN'T JUST SAY HE'D CHANGED HIS MIND!

NO. =SNIFF= SO HE MADE UP ALL THESE **HORRIBLE** STORIES ABOUT ME...

THAT I WAS A **WITCH**, AND THAT I'D **FORCED** HIM TO MARRY ME WITH **MAGIC SPELLS**, AND I WAS HAVING AFFAIRS WITH **5 MEN**, INCLUDING MY OWN **BROTHER!**

THERE, THERE, DEAR. WE ALL KNEW THEY WERE LIES...

GROSS LIES.

OO HOO HOO!

BUT YOU DIDN'T SAY ANYTHING?

NO ONE SAID ANYTHING!

HE WAS THE KING...

SO ANNE GOT THE CHOP...

AND IN CAME WIFE NUMBER 3...

JANE SEYMOUR!

CORPSE TALK "I'D MUCH RATHER BE SEWING."

HUH? WHAT'S THAT?

OH, SORRY. IS IT MY TURN? I'M JUST ON A TRICKY STITCH HERE...

JANE, YOU WERE MARRYING A MAN WHO HAD JUST **KILLED** HIS WIFE! WEREN'T YOU AFRAID?

IN ALL HONESTY, I WAS **TERRIFIED!**

BUT I COULDN'T REALLY SAY NO, COULD I? ANYWAY, SO LONG AS I COULD POP OUT A **BOY**, I'D BE FINE...

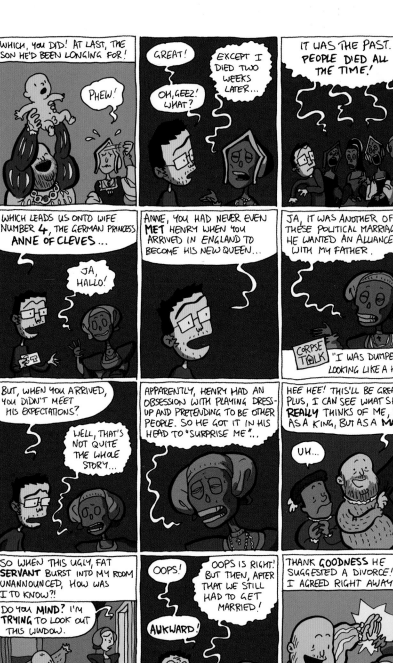

WELL, OKAY, LIKE, AT FIRST, I LIKED ALL THE JEWELLERY AND THE, LIKE, ATTENTION...

CORPSE TALK "DON'T HATE ME 'COS I'M PRETTY!"

OMG! I WAS JUST, LIKE, TOTALLY **POOR** BEFORE!

BUT MY UNCLE WAS, LIKE, TOTALLY THE DUKE OF NORFOLK. HE ARRANGED FOR ME TO COME TO COURT AND LIKE, TOTALLY MEET THE KING.

AND SO, IF **YOU** MARRIED THE KING, YOUR UNCLE WOULD ALSO BECOME MORE POWERFUL.

...

OMG! THAT'S TOTALLY IT!

THAT EXPLAINS WHY HE WAS ALL LIKE "BE NICE TO THE KING" AND "ACT LIKE YOU THINK HE'S GREAT" AND "DON'T MENTION HIS BIG BELLY."

SO THE KING THOUGHT YOU WERE WONDERFUL. YOU MADE HIM FEEL YOUNG AND LOVED AGAIN.

OKAY, WELL... HERE'S, LIKE, THE THING. BEFORE, I LIVED AT MY AUNT'S HOUSE. SHE WAS TOTALLY OLD AND LIKE, TOTALLY DEAF.

I USED TO LIKE, TOTALLY SNEAK BOYFRIENDS IN THERE ALL THE TIME...

UH-OH! THIS DOESN'T SOUND GOOD...

WELL, THERE WAS LIKE, THIS **GUY**...

THOMAS CULPEPPER! HE WAS ONE OF THE YOUNG MEN AT COURT. HE JUST LOOKED SO **CUTE** IN HIS TIGHTS AND THOSE LITTLE POOFY LEG THINGS...

SO YOU STARTED HAVING AN AFFAIR.

AND THE KING FOUND OUT.

...

I WAS LIKE, TOTALLY IN THE MIDDLE OF A DANCING LESSON WHEN THEY ARRESTED ME.

STEPPIN' OUT ON THE KING, THAT'S **HIGH TREASON**! PLUS, LOOK AT WHAT HAPPENED TO THE **OTHERS**! WHAT **WERE** YOU **THINKING**!

HENRY WAS HEARTBROKEN! (AFTER HAVING YOUR HEAD CUT OFF.) BUT, AMAZINGLY, IT STILL DIDN'T PUT HIM OFF GETTING MARRIED! HE DECIDED **YOU** WOULD BE HIS NEXT BRIDE, **KATHERINE PARR**...

I DIDN'T HAVE MUCH CHOICE IN THE MATTER. I'D ALREADY HAD **TWO** POLITICAL MARRIAGES, AND WAS LOOKING FORWARD TO MARRYING MY TRUE LOVE...

CORPSE TALK "I KEPT MY HEAD, AND MADE SMALL TALK INSTEAD."

BY THIS POINT, HE WAS TERRIBLY FAT, AND HE HAD AN AWFUL LEG WOUND THAT WOULDN'T HEAL. I KEPT HIM ENTERTAINED WITH DEBATES AN—

BORING!

HEY! AT LEAST I **SURVIVED**!

OH, RIGHT! BY, LIKE, TOTALLY DISCUSSING **POLITICS**! WISH I'D THOUGHT OF THAT!

WELL, MAYBE IF YOU WEREN'T SO **DUMB**, YOU WOULD HAVE!

OH, YOU DID **NOT** JUST SAY THAT! IT IS **ON**!

So Edward sent a huge army to **KILL** you and **SUBDUE** Scotland!

But first he had to **FIND** me! My smaller, lighter army meant I could watch and wait until the perfect opportunity to attack.

And that opportunity came when they tried to cross over **STIRLING BRIDGE**...

The English army was bigger and better equipped, but I had a plan to turn that against them. I waited until most of them had crossed the bridge...

...And then we attacked!

THE SCOTS!

GET THEM!

GET IN LINE!

GET OUT OF MY WAY!

AAAAAAAAAAAH!

BRIDGE

HILL

MARSHY GROUND

Their heavily armoured knights got stuck in the swamp, and the Scots picked them off with extra-long spears.

The English tried to retreat across the bridge while their reinforcements tried to charge. It was **MAYHEM!**

ATTACK!

RETREAT!

GET OFF MY FOOT!

The bridge **COLLAPSED** under all their weight, and their heavy armour pulled them down and **DROWNED** them!

We were especially pleased to have killed a guy called **HUGH DE CRESSINGHAM**. He was in charge of stealing all the Scots' **MONEY**.

THE ROTTER!

We **SKINNED** him and every soldier got a piece!

ONE FOR YOU... ONE FOR YOU...

CAN I GET AN EXTRA PIECE? IT'S FOR MY DAUGHTER...

You were knighted and named "**HIGH GUARDIAN OF SCOTLAND.**" You were riding high!

UNTIL I GOT CAPTURED...

I was put on trial as a traitor, but I said 'How could I be a traitor to Edward when he was never my true king?'

I was sentenced to be **HANGED, DRAWN AND QUARTERED!** It was the most torturous mode of execution they had!

First they **HUNG** me until I was almost, but not quite, dead...

WOO! STRING 'IM UP!

Then they cut open my stomach, **DREW** out my **GUTS**, and set them on fire.

OH, YEAH? IS THIS THE BEST YOU CAN DO?!

I'VE HAD WORSE HEARTBURN!

And then they cut off my head.

AND CUT YOU INTO QUARTERS!

AND CUT ME INTO QUARTERS...

THUMP!

PULL YOURSELF TOGETHER, MAN!

GEORGE WASHINGTON CARVER

THIS WEEK, MY GUEST IS A BRILLIANT SCIENTIST AND INVENTOR, WHO USED HIS DEEP LOVE OF NATURE TO IMPROVE THE LIVES OF MILLIONS. IT'S **THE PLANT WHISPERER**, GEORGE WASHINGTON CARVER!

PROFESSOR CARVER, YOU DEVELOPED YOUR LOVE OF PLANTS AT A VERY EARLY AGE.

YES, I USED TO GO WALKING IN THE WOODS NEAR THE FARM WHERE I LIVED...

I WANTED TO KNOW THE NAMES OF EVERY **STONE** AND **FLOWER** AND **INSECT** AND **BIRD** AND **BEAST**. I WANTED TO KNOW WHERE IT GOT ITS **COLOUR**, WHERE IT GOT ITS **LIFE** – BUT THERE WAS NO ONE TO TELL ME.

COULDN'T YOU ASK YOUR PARENTS?

I NEVER KNEW THEM.

MY PARENTS WERE **SLAVES** IN AMERICA– BELONGING TO A FARMER CALLED MOSES CARVER.

POPPA DIED BEFORE I WAS BORN. MY MOMMA AND I GOT **STOLEN** BY **SLAVE RAIDERS** WHEN I WAS JUST A BABY.

MR CARVER TRADED A **HORSE** TO GET ME BACK, BUT THEY'D ALREADY **SOLD** MY MOMMA. I NEVER SAW HER AGAIN.

I STAYED ON AT CARVER'S FARM, AND IT WAS THERE THAT I DISCOVERED I COULD USE MY **PLANT POWERS** TO HELP PEOPLE OUT!

WITH ALL THE TIME I SPENT TALKING TO THE PLANTS, I KNEW A LOT ABOUT WHAT THEY LIKED AND HOW TO HELP THEM GROW.

SO I KNEW HOW TO HELP OUT FOLKS IF THEY HAD SICK PLANTS. THEY USED TO CALL ME THE **PLANT DOCTOR**!

I WANTED TO KEEP ON LEARNING, BUT THEY WOULDN'T ALLOW BLACK FOLKS TO STUDY AT THE LOCAL SCHOOL. SO I SET OFF ON FOOT TO FIND ONE THAT DID!

THAT WAS HOW I MET MISS **MARIAH WATKINS**. SHE WAS A NICE LADY WHO OWNED THE BARN I HAD BEEN SLEEPING IN...

I NEVER FORGOT WHAT SHE SAID TO ME...

YOU MUST LEARN ALL YOU CAN, THEN GO BACK OUT INTO THE WORLD AND GIVE YOUR LEARNING BACK TO THE PEOPLE.

WHICH YOU DID, BECOMING A PROFESSOR OF **BOTANY**. AND IT WASN'T LONG BEFORE YOU FOUND SOME MORE **PLANT PROBLEMS** TO HELP WITH...

WELL, AT THAT TIME THERE WAS A BIG PROBLEM IN THE SOUTH. YOU SEE, ALL THE BLACK FOLKS THAT USED TO BE SLAVES WERE NOW FREE FARMERS.

WHICH **SHOULD** HAVE BEEN GREAT, EXCEPT THAT THEY ONLY HAD EXPERIENCE WITH GROWING COTTON.

AND COTTON **DEPLETES** THE SOIL, SO AFTER A FEW YEARS THERE'S NO NUTRIENTS LEFT AND THE CROPS ALL DIE.

I REALISED THEY COULD PLANT **OTHER** CROPS, THINGS THAT NATIVELY GROW IN THE SOUTH, THAT WOULD PUT NUTRIENTS **BACK INTO** THE SOIL.

CROPS LIKE **PEANUTS!**

I HAD A LITTLE WAGON THAT I DROVE AROUND, TEACHING FOLKS HOW TO USE THIS **CROP ROTATION SYSTEM.**

SOON PEOPLE ALL OVER THE SOUTH WERE GROWING PEANUTS! ONLY ONE PROBLEM...

NO ONE **WANTS** ALL THESE PEANUTS! WHAT AM I GOING TO **DO** WITH THEM?!

UH.... **EAT** THEM?

THAT'S THE THING. BACK THEN, PEOPLE DIDN'T EAT PEANUTS! SO I GOT IN THE LAB AND STARTED **INVENTING**...

I DISCOVERED OVER **300** PEANUT INVENTIONS, INCLUDING: PEANUT INK, PEANUT SOAP, PEANUT MILK, PEANUT CHEESE, PEANUT COFFEE, PEANUT MAYONNAISE AND PEANUT PEPPER.

SIP

OKAY, SOME OF THEM WERE PRETTY GROSS. BUT THERE WAS **ONE** PEANUT INVENTION THAT WAS **REALLY** POPULAR...

WAA?!

WAIT, YOU MEAN **YOU'RE** THE REASON WE EAT PEANUT BUTTER?

MIND... **BLOWN!**

AND I DIDN'T STOP WITH PEANUTS. I ALSO DISCOVERED THINGS YOU COULD MAKE FROM **OTHER** HELPFUL PLANTS, LIKE RUBBER FROM SWEET POTATOES, OR HIGHWAY PAVING FROM PECANS...

WOW — ALL THESE INVENTIONS MUST'VE MADE YOU REALLY **RICH!**

HEH HEH. RICH IN **SPIRIT** MAYBE, BUT NOT IN MONEY. I NEVER REALLY CARED ABOUT THAT.

THOMAS EDISON, THE FAMOUS INVENTOR OF THE LIGHT BULB, WANTED TO PAY ME **BIG BUCKS** TO MAKE INVENTIONS FOR HIM...

BUT HE WANTED TO KEEP THEM ALL FOR HIMSELF, AND MAKE PEOPLE **PAY** TO USE THEM.

I BELIEVED MY DISCOVERIES WERE A **GIFT FROM GOD,** TALKING TO ME THROUGH HIS PLANTS. YOU CAN'T **SELL** SOMETHING LIKE THAT!

WELL, LET'S ALL GIVE THANKS FOR THE WONDERFUL GIFT OF PEANUT BUTTER!

OOH, THANK YOU, THANK YOU, OM NOM NOM NOM...

NOT AGAIN! WE WENT TO THE BEACH TO CELEBRATE THE END OF THE SERIES AND NOW IT'S TIME TO HEAD BACK TO THE GRAVEYARD. BUT IT'S GETTING NEAR DAWN – SOON THE SUN WILL BE UP AND THE LIVING WILL START ARRIVING. I HOPE YOU CAN REMEMBER WHO'S WHO BECAUSE YOU NEED TO GIVE A ROLL-CALL TO GET THEM ALL BACK ON THE CORPSE COACH!